Faith

ISBN 978-1-0980-5399-4 (paperback)
ISBN 978-1-0980-5400-7 (hardcover)
ISBN 978-1-0980-5401-4 (digital)

Christian Faith Publishing, Inc.
832 Park Avenue
Meadville, PA 16335
www.christianfaithpublishing.com

Printed in the United States of America

Faith

Hi Tony,

I loved your segment on African American Childrens books and I thought it would be awesome if you could read this 1st time Authors book to your children.

I love CBS News, and watch it all the time,

Thank You,

Sandra Jackson-Hines

Sandra Jackson-Hines

A little girl named **Faith** realizes that she is seeing the same numbers over and over again. She wants to know, why? And, what does it mean?

Throughout her journey she finds out what God is trying to tell her.

There was a young girl named

Faith who was on her way to school.

While in her math class, the teacher put a math example on the blackboard.

$$9 + 23 =$$

"Does anyone know the answer?" the teacher asked.

Everyone was giving the wrong answer.

9 + 23 =

4

Suddenly **Faith** raised her hand and shouted, "Thirty-two!"

"Yes, **Faith**, very good," the teacher said.

Faith was so excited because she was the only one in her class that gave the right answer.

Faith was so happy she skipped all the way home.

Faith ran into her mom's arms and gave her the *good news*.

"Hey, Mom, I was the only one in class today that gave the right answer."

Faith's mom said, "You were so good in school. Tonight I will read you a bedtime story after we eat dinner."

Faith took her bath…

put on her pj's…

and went to bed.

She waited…and waited. "Mom, Mom!" she cried out.

"You promised its **9:23**"

When **Faith** said "**923**," she remembered those were the same numbers in her math class at school.

She pointed to the clock. "Look, Mom, look! Look the numbers."

Faith's mom laughed and said, "Okay, okay, I know you're ready for your story. Let's get going."

The next day was Saturday. Faith was ready to have fun. Mom and Dad were taking Faith to the aquarium. When they got there, Faith saw a big sign that read.

Sea Lion Show

Starts

at

9:23

She pointed to the sign. "Mom, Dad, look."

"I know, honey. You're so excited to see the show. Let's go in," Dad said.

They enjoyed their day at the aquarium and stopped for pizza at their favorite restaurant.

Faith's favorite thing about pizza was the gooey cheese on top. They ate 'til they couldn't eat any more. When the waitress came to give Dad the check, the total was $**9.23**.

Faith's dad paid the bill, not knowing anything about the numbers.

"Okay, let's get in the car," Dad said. "We have church early in the morning."

Everyone got in the car, and they went home.

When they got to church the next day, the pastor was teaching about believing God can do all things. Even though we don't see him, he is working on our problems day and night. God can make you happy when you're sad. He can make you feel better when you are sick. He will help you in any way when you pray and ask him.

The pastor said, "Open your Bible, and in the book of Mark chapter **9** verse **23,** it says all things are possible to him that believe."

Faith's eyes popped open so wide, and she pulled on Mom's skirt. "Mom, Mom, Mom!"

"Shhh," Mom said. "The pastor is speaking."

"But, Mom," **Faith** whispered, "it's the numbers again—**923**."

Mom said, "**Faith**, you're right. The whole time, God was trying to tell us to just believe and trust in him and that anything is possible."

About the Author

Sandra Jackson-Hines resides in Connecticut with her husband. She enjoys teaching and spending time with the children at her church.

This book is based on a true story.

Her hope is to show children and adults that God is always trying to get our attention. But it is up to us to listen.

Sjacksonhines@gmail.com

CPSIA information can be obtained
at www.ICGtesting.com
Printed in the USA
BVHW022244220221
600819BV00002B/3